The Smart Girl's Guide To Surviving Her Twenties

The Smart Girl's Guide To Surviving Her Twenties

COURTNEY LIVINGSTON

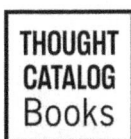

THOUGHT
CATALOG
Books

BROOKLYN, NY

THOUGHT
CATALOG
Books

Collective
World

Published by Thought Catalog Books, a publishing house owned by The Thought & Expression Co., Williamsburg, Brooklyn.

First edition, 2017

ISBN: 978-1945796517

Printed and bound in the United States.

10 9 8 7 6 5 4 3 2 1

To Katie, the smartest girl I know.

Contents

Foreword		1
1.	Career	3
2.	Minimalism	15
3.	Finances	25
4.	Fitness	33
5.	Nutrition	43
6.	Relationships	55
7.	Travel	67
About the Author		75
You Might Also Like...		77

Foreword

Congratulations. You've made it to your twenties.

Welcome to the world of college graduations, careers, travels, new friendships, and so. much. more.

It's exciting, this non-teenage world where you're set free from the rigidness of childhood but not yet swayed by the ways of the world.

It's also pretty scary. And maybe a little bit terrifying. How are you supposed to know what to do? How will you survive?

Well, I've got a secret for you.

It's not as hard as it seems.

It all starts with habits. Daily, weekly, moment by moment habits. You see, the habits you develop now will set yourself up for success later in life. So we're going to go through this new adventure together to make sure you're ready to take on this next decade of your life.

If you're already well into your twenties, not to worry, this book is for you too. Whether you're a college gal, a young professional, or a late bloomer ready to crawl out of your parents' basement, this book's got you covered.

The path you choose now will have a huge payoff later. The choices you make in your twenties are the biggest investment you'll ever make. We haven't a moment to lose. So let's get started, shall we?

1

Career

I still remember lying on my bed at 11 o'clock at night, staring at a blank Word document, hands poised to type, and clicking from that Word document over to Pinterest. Because Pinterest is so much more exciting than writing a paper that was due at midnight.

The minutes ticked on. Perspiration beaded on my forehead. I reached into the bowl of popcorn squished in between my thighs and shoved a handful into my mouth. The popcorn spilled all over me as the handful was entirely too big to fit into my mouth. I then proceeded to hop off my bed, wash the butter off my face, clean up the spilled popcorn, and check social media, all before going back to my position in bed, laptop open and ready.

The battery light blinked. Just 29% left. I glanced over at my roommate, who lay soundlessly asleep. She had been waiting for me to write this paper so we could go outside and hang with our group of friends, but unfortunately, the procrastinator in me had come to life, allowing me to do everything but write this paper. The alarm clock perched on my bookshelf flashed, signaling the dawning of a new minute.

And then the words came.

They flooded out of my fingers, filling up the pages of that blank Word document. I typed and quoted and added in those footnotes and threw together citations. Five minutes left. Five minutes to edit this paper. I read and rewrote and fixed all those squiggly, red-underlined words. One minute left. I opened the submissions tab, uploaded my paper, and clicked submit.

And the clock turned to midnight.

Yet another assignment turned in, just at the nick of time. The Queen of Procrastination had ruled once again.

I'm sure I'm not the only one who has had this experience. If you've ever been a college student, then you've probably been there too. And if you're currently a college student, then maybe I just described your night. Procrastination is a way of life in the college world.

But at some point, that graduation date comes and you walk across a stage, accepting your (hard-earned?) diploma.

And real life begins.

A life where procrastination will get you fired. A life where putting things off can affect your entire future. A life where staying up till late into the night scrolling the Internet will leave you drained and unable to function come morning.

It's best to put the procrastination habits behind you once you cross that stage. Or better yet, even before you cross the stage if you haven't done so already.

After earning that degree which you lost so many hours of sleep over and paid an exorbitant amount of money for, it's time to get to work.

It's time to be independent, to find your dream job, and to put your education to use.

It's time to start your career.

I remember my first year of teaching like it was yesterday. I had spent four years getting that elementary education degree, and I was so nervous about having my own classroom. But after just a few weeks of teaching, I realized I had no idea what I was doing. I thought I could still manage both my career and a side job. I was stuck in that college girl mindset where going to school and working was a normal thing to do. I didn't realize that I needed to put my side job to rest and focus on my career. In addition to that, I was determined to do all of my work while I was on the clock, and I refused to take any work home.

I had heard horror stories of how teachers spent hours grading papers at home, and I was terrified I would let my job overtake my life. So I purposefully strived to work as fast I could to get ahead and go against the grain of rumors I had heard.

But sadly, I only hurt myself in the process. In my obsession with working nonstop on the clock without regards to anyone around me, I made mistakes. Mistakes that could have been avoided if I had only asked for help. I holed myself in rather than reaching out, and by the end of my first year, I was over this whole teaching thing.

I began to wonder why I had chosen to get my degree in such an all-consuming field. I complained that none of my coworkers helped me, I was swamped with paperwork, and I couldn't control my students. I felt like I could never get ahead, and I would never succeed. And unsurprisingly, I wasn't asked back for the second year.

So I went back to the drawing board. AKA, I started reapplying. At this point, I was a pro at the whole resumé, application, and interview deal. And I had experience now which put me on top of the slush pile.

With a year of work under my belt, I knew exactly what type of teaching job I now wanted. I wasn't going to take just any job. I had specifics, and I was willing to go wherever it took to find the job I wanted.

Just days after packing up my classroom, I was sitting in the Bahamas enjoying my first week of summer vacation. My resumés had been sent out long before the school year ended, I had had a few interviews, and follow-up phone calls had been made. I randomly decided to check my email while chilling on my balcony, the ocean breeze blowing around me, and low and behold, I had an offer for a contract at my dream school. This school was everything I was looking for in a job, so I decided to take a leap of faith, move away from the state I had lived my entire life in, and take this new job.

And I'm so glad I did. I learned from what I did wrong in my first year and used it to fuel my second year of teaching. I sought out help and encouragement from others. I didn't race to beat the clock, and I didn't mind staying a few minutes late off the clock. I became involved. I asked questions. Lots and lots of questions. And as my second year drew to a close, I was asked to return and was given raving performance reviews.

If you fail in the beginning of your career, life isn't over. You may not succeed the first time or the second time, but that doesn't give you an excuse to give up. If you get fired, laid off, or end up hating your workplace, find a new job. The more experience you have, the more you know what you want out of work. As I like to say, if you don't like where you're at, move; you're not a tree. Focus on your strengths and become even stronger. Pinpoint weaknesses and figure out a way to work through those areas. Don't give up. Remember, our twenties are for growth, and growth has to start somewhere.

If you are unsatisfied with your job, your pay grade, or your status, don't be afraid to go back to school. Use that paycheck and put it towards furthering your education. There are countless options available for online classes, night classes, and all sorts of programs to help you achieve higher goals.

Figure out what your goals are and allow them to guide you throughout the coming years. I'm not talking relationship, travel, or bucket list goals. I'm talking work and educational goals. Want to have your master's degree by the time you're 24? Work out a path to get it. Want to have your doctorate by 27? Start working towards it. Setting goals is the best way to help you visualize your future and gives you something to strive for.

Without goals, your life will slip right by you. Don't wake up when you're thirty with nothing but a laundry list of failed opportunities to show for it. Know what you want, and go out and grab it.

Once we graduate college, trade school, or whatever we trained to do, working at the local coffee shop just isn't going to cut it. As nice as it is to work a flexible, part-time job, we eventually have to pursue a full-time position.

But where do we start?

Finding your dream job is no easy task. It takes research, connections, and lots of determination.

To help you feel prepared as you start this job search of yours, we're going to go through the basic steps required to find your dream job. These steps will guide you through what to do as you get ready to move on to the post-college portion of your life.

So roll those shoulders back, take a deep breath, and saddle up some self-confidence. It's go time.

Step 1: Look The Part

Use some of that grad money of yours and buy yourself a pair of dress pants and a dress shirt. It's best to look professional and not like you just left behind your beloved sorority house or finished up a summer as a camp counselor. Those grown-up stores you used to pay no mind to as you wandered through the mall? You might want to check them out.

It's best to leave those funky teen stores behind you for good. You're in your twenties now, and if you want potential employers and future colleagues to see you as a capable adult, you have to dress like one.

So fix your hair and put on your big-girl makeup. It's time to job hunt.

Step 2: Create A Resumé

Crank up your laptop, open up a resumé template, and get to work. This is your chance to make yourself shine. Your potential employer has loads of resumés to thumb through, and yours needs to stand out.

What special skills do you have? Write about them. If you don't have any particular skills related to your job field, be general and talk about your leadership capabilities, how you're a self-starter, or how you're an excellent communicator.

Make sure you put down all of your past work experience. Your employer wants to see that you have good work ethic, so the longer the list, the better you look.

Before sending this resumé out, have others read it. Have that old favorite professor check it over to make sure it's perfect. Ask professionals in your future job field for tips on how to make it better. You want to make sure you are selling the best parts about you and not leaving anything important out.

Once you've got this resumé perfect, print it out on resumé

paper and put on those new dress clothes. It's time to drop those babies off.

And we're going to drop them off in person. After filling out the accompanying applications, go to each place you applied to and ask to see your would-be boss. Hand them your resumé and introduce yourself, expressing your interest in the job you are applying for. If the boss isn't there, leave your resumé, and go back during a time when they are there.

Now it's time to wait. If a full day goes by with no callbacks, give them a call. And another one. And another one. Until you get an interview.

Step 3: The Interview

Once you land an interview, it's important to do your homework. Who will you be interviewing with? What type of questions will be asked? This is when Google will become your best friend. Look up sample interview questions that relate to your job field, and study, study, study. Have your roommate interview you. Get the nervous, stutter-filled answers out before you even go in.

This is your chance to present to them why you're the best person for the job.

Make sure you show up to your interview at least five minutes early. Look professional and dress for the job you want. Bring a portfolio of work-related ideas to show and another copy of your resumé. If you have a copy of the application you filled out, bring that as well. There's a good chance your interviewer will ask you questions related to the answers on your application.

When you're in the interview, be calm and outgoing. When they ask you questions, think before speaking. There's no reason to spill out a fast answer you didn't take the time to think through. And it's good etiquette to repeat the question in your answer. I've listed five common interview questions that you need to make sure you have an answer to prior to arriving at your interview.

- *Can you tell me a little bit about yourself?*
- *Why should we hire you?*
- *What do you consider to be your weaknesses? Strengths?*
- *Tell me about a challenge or conflict you faced at work and how you dealt with it.*
- *Do you have any questions for us?*

When they ask you if you have any questions about the company, make sure you are prepared to fill their ears with thought-out questions. This shows that you have taken the time to learn about the company and are interested in learning more about them.

Step 4: Wait

Welcome to the dreaded purgatory between ending your interview and waiting to hear back. Sometimes you'll hear back the same day and other times it could be weeks. Don't be afraid to call back to check on the status of their decision, but try not to pester too much. And don't place all of your eggs into one basket. Try to land as many interviews as you can. This strengthens your chances of finding a job and could give you options if you are offered multiple positions.

Step 5: Rejoice Or Move On

Once you get that call offering you your dream job, congrats! Celebrate, call all of your college buddies to let them know this exciting news, and get ready for this new era of your life.

If you've waited a few months and still can't seem to find a job in your area of expertise, it might be time to consider applying for jobs in a new geographical area. There's no reason to stay in one place and settle for a less than ideal job just because you can't find one in your hometown or in the town you so badly want to live in.

Being in our twenties is a time of growth and change, and sometimes moving somewhere out of our comfort zone is the only way we can find success in our fields.

Moving somewhere new challenges us to grow. I know it can be tempting to move back to the home you grew up in, reconnect with old friends, and live rent-free in your childhood room for a little while, but doing so will only cause you to take steps backward rather than steps forward.

And we want to be taking steps forward.

Remember, this book is called the smart girl's guide to being in her twenties. Not the lazy, mooching, dependent-on-her-parents, too-afraid-to-start-fresh girl's guide to being in her twenties.

Don't just bebop your way through your first decade of adulthood. Put aside the college girl and welcome in this new, young, professional twenty-something lady. (Eek, I know, the word lady sounds so old, but it's okay; own it!) You can do it. You can get that job, get that promotion, and earn that degree. Don't let anyone or any circumstance stop you. It's your life, your decade, and your golden window of opportunity. Don't let it pass without giving it everything you've got.

2

Minimalism

I stared at my closet, feeling utterly overwhelmed by all of the junk I had managed to accumulate. I was twenty-two and in between teaching jobs. I had just finished my first year of teaching and was preparing to move so I could start my new job in a new state. We rented a small trailer to help us move, so, consequently, we could only bring a limited number of items with us. The rest had to go.

As I stared at my closet, I realized that in the three short years that I had been in my twenties, I had acquired endless amounts of crap—AKA clothes, decorations, and possessions—that I thought would bring me happiness. Granted, all of the junk wasn't mine. A big load of it belonged to my husband who has slight packrat tendencies, but nonetheless, the amount of stuff we had accumulated was mind-boggling.

So we had to clear it out. First went the gun safe filled with my husband's precious guns. Our new apartment wouldn't allow guns on the premises. Next came our clothes. I would need a separate moving truck to haul all of the clothes from one state to another, so I decided to sell a good chunk of my wardrobe. Then came the books, the knickknacks, the jars of perfume laid out on my dresser, the picture frames scattered throughout the house, the vases, the coffee mugs (so. many. coffee. mugs.), the throw rugs, the candles, etcetera, etcetera.

Since I was moving from a regular house to a townhouse, I had to do a bit of downsizing. The number one question I asked myself was: Do I really need this? The answer was usually, no, I do not need this iced tea maker or salad dressing mixer. (And yes, I still eat salad, but what twenty-something has time to make their own dressing?) My rule was if I hadn't used it in a year, I probably wouldn't be using it anytime soon. So it got tossed into the donations pile.

Once my possessions had been thoroughly sorted through, we loaded up the trucks and headed to our new home. Our townhouse was a lot smaller than our old home but much more manageable in terms of decorating (and cleaning!). It was a simple two-story home squished in between a row of other homes and contained the basics of what one needs in a home. There was no fancy yard, no screened-in porch, no expansive dining room, and only one bathroom. This was quite the opposite from where we lived before, but I was ready for a change. After all, keeping up with an expansive house and yard was tiring and quite taxing on the wallet, so I was reading for something different.

As I moved into this new living space, I was determined not to let my possessions oppress me. Possessions were no longer going to rule over my desires. I now knew where those possessions ended up—being sold in a trash bag for a few bucks or donated to the local thrift store. I was determined to start fresh with the purpose of ridding myself of life's excess so I could reapply my resources to other areas of life.

As I began to lay down some roots in this new town I was living in, I started incorporating the question of "Do I really need this?" into all areas of life.

When I went grocery shopping, I went with a list of full of things I only needed for that week. My refrigerator began to look a lot less full, and I was no longer throwing away uneaten leftovers or forgotten veggies. I had just what I needed, and I didn't need a plethora of options every time I opened up the fridge.

When I went clothes shopping, I found myself buying less and less until I ultimately stopped going recreational shopping altogether. I started pulling things out of my closet I had forgotten about and became creative with mixing and matching outfits. If I wore something twice in a two-week period, I stopped caring. Chances are, most people didn't notice that type of thing anyway. I was going wear the clothes I owned and loved, unashamedly.

Soon my home became less stressful. I no longer had a "junk drawer" or a garage filled with stuff I rarely used. It took just a few minutes to clean up my house compared to the hours it would take when I had needless possessions scattered throughout.

This stress-free lifestyle led my husband and me to become more productive. My husband finished his Master's degree, and I wrote a book—both huge goals that had been lingering over our heads that we had been inching our way towards.

This new lifestyle freed up our mental space and inspired us to charge after our goals with everything in us.

We also freed ourselves up financially. By not wasting money on things we didn't truly need, we were able to pay for my husband's degree with cash. We were able to take a vacation without having to dip into our savings. When we needed to make a purchase, we were able to purchase high-quality items that would last a long time. This lifestyle was changing our entire way of life.

Eventually, my question of "Do I really need this?" changed to "Will this add value to my life?"

Slowly but surely, I was becoming a minimalist.

Minimalism is a lifestyle that allows us to question the things that add value to our lives. By clearing the clutter out of our lives, we can make way for what's most important: relationships, growth, health, passion, and contribution.

Embracing minimalism doesn't mean you have to put a set of restrictions on yourself as to what you can or can't own. Rather, minimalism offers us a way to live with more time, money, and freedom to live a meaningful life.

As Colin Wright put it, "We don't get bonus points when we die for owning more stuff than the other guy, nor do we get a trophy for owning less than someone else. We do get to smile on our deathbeds if we enjoyed the heck out of life, however, so that's what I plan to focus on."

Below are three steps to help you minimize your life and

embrace the minimalist mindset. It's best to start minimizing now in your twenties so you can develop life-long habits that will spread throughout all areas of your life.

Step 1: De-clutter

Clutter keeps you tied to the past. When you look around and are reminded of things of the past, this forces your mind to reminisce, conjuring up past solutions to old thought processes. When our minds are tied to the past, this prevents us from making space for new thoughts and ideas. While it's sad to put away old photos and things that remind us of our high school glory days and college passions, in order to grow it is imperative that we make room for what is to come.

Minimizing our living space, our workspace, and our life in general forces us to recognize the problems of today and create solutions for tomorrow.

We must release the past to create a better tomorrow.

Put the things most important to you in a box for safekeeping and let the rest go. The walls around you should help spark your creativity, feed your passions, and allow your mind to run free.

Don't let emotional attachments to things take over your mental space and inhibit your ability to be productive.

As Joshua Becker says in his book, *The More of Less*, "Our excessive possessions are not making us happy. Even worse, they are taking us away from the things that do. Once we let go of the things that don't matter, we are free to pursue all the things that really do matter."

Step 2: Stop Buying Stuff

John Ruskin, a 19th-century art critic, once wrote, "Every increased possession loads us with a new weariness."

Every time we acquire something, we are now tasked with the responsibility to take care of said thing and make sure it brings us the most amount of happiness it possible can. Whether it's a new shirt, a new pair of shoes, a new car, or a new house, the things we possess require our attention and time, whether it be through researching, shopping, cleaning, organizing, repairing, replacing, reselling, or simply working to make the money to buy it in the first place. It taxes us. It steals our time. The prospect of acquiring this new thing is exciting, and we think it just might make us happy, but that is simply an illusion. The more stuff we own, the more our stuff owns us.

A wise teacher once said, "For where your treasure is, there your heart will be also."

This means that our hearts will gravitate towards what we care about most.

I still remember when I got my first cell phone at the ripe old age of seventeen. (Yes, I was indeed the last of my friends to get one!) Because I had waited years to finally own a cell phone, I treasured this phone like nothing else. It was a pink touch screen phone and I was so very proud of it. However, a week or two after acquiring this precious phone, I decided to go for a swim at my grandmother's house. I wrapped my phone up tightly in a towel so it wouldn't get wet before proceeding to dive into the pool.

A few minutes later, my grandmother came strolling out of the house. She saw the pile of wadded up towels and proceeded to shake them out and hang them to dry. Before I realized what was about to happen, my grandma shook out my towel, and my phone went skidding across the concrete. I quickly jumped out of the pool, screaming "NOOOOO!" in the process, before picking up my phone and finding a series of scratches across the front of it.

My beautiful new phone was now marred and my heart was crushed. I knew that I would have to live with this scratched up phone for the next two years, and I was livid.

Over time, stories similar to this one seemed to rule my life. I'd have a necklace that meant the world to me and it would fall down the sink when I tried to put it on. I would wreck my new-to-me car the first week of college, and I would misplace the watch my mother gave to me on my twentieth birthday just weeks before she was diagnosed with cancer (although I did find it under the couch two years later when I moved!)

It seemed as though I always lost or broke the things that were most valuable to me. But therein lies the problem. Each of those "things" was a possession. They weren't people, and they weren't experiences. They were valuables that were intended to bring me happiness but ultimately brought me great displeasure.

Ruskin was right. Possessions bring a whopping load of weariness along with them.

So I stopped caring about possessions. Now that's a difficult thing to do when the world tells us that our stuff is what defines us and that we can't be happy without acquiring new things. This whole "not caring" deal wasn't easy, and it still isn't. But once you reach a point in your life where your heart doesn't belong to your things, you will feel much freer and happier.

Flash forward a few years. I was loading up my car with a bunch of teenagers as we were driving back home from a week of church camp that I had chaperoned. Sleeping bags, pillows, blankets, and suitcases blocked my back window, and I couldn't see out of it. As I was backing out of my parking spot, I hit a giant rock. Quickly hopping out of my car, I soon realized the plastic tire cover on the back of my car now had a crack in it thanks to that big rock.

I had every reason to freak out. I couldn't see where I was going. This car was less than a year old. Someone who was standing around should have warned me above this rock.

But instead of freaking out, I took a deep breath, rolled my shoulders back, and shrugged. I looked at my husband to see his reaction, half expecting him to freak out, but he just rubbed my back and said it was no big deal. It was just a tire cover, and it wasn't even entirely broken, just cracked. It would be okay.

This was a moment that I will never forget. It was a turning point for us. This moment showed me that we had both gotten to a point where stuff didn't matter. It was just a car, just a thing, just a possession. And my possessions didn't own me. Possessions didn't rule my happiness.

The wise teacher was right. Focus on what matters, and when something breaks or loses its zeal, it won't take away from your joy. Don't let buying and owning stuff rule your happiness.

> *"When we begin to invest our money, time, and lives into more meaningful things like relationships, social causes, or raising our children, our hearts will be drawn to those things because that is where our life investment is going."*
> —Joshua Becker

Step 3: Give Back

Once you've mastered (or at least started working towards) steps one and two, you will soon find yourself with more resources than you had before. Minimalism provides you with the opportunity to not only save money but also to further the causes that you believe in. While it's great to invest our money, we also need to make sure we are giving back and not just lording over our resources, for that could lead us into greedy, unhealthy habits that will not benefit anyone.

So take a portion of your means and find a way to give back. My way of doing this is contributing financially to my local church. My local church, in turn, contributes to the local community and to our members in myriad ways. By contributing to my church, I am furthering my beliefs, helping those in need, and supporting my pastor so he can lead our church.

Choose what matters most to you and give back accordingly. If you want to help people in Africa afford wells so they can have clean water, then do it. If you want to support environmental education in Central America, then support it. If you want that little niece of yours to be able to play piano, then pay for the lessons.

Giving back will look differently for us all, but the most important thing is that we are using our resources to help others.

So forget about stuff. Happiness is not found in square footage, having all the latest brands, or in keeping up with those around us. Happiness is found in filling our lives with meaningful experiences. Keyword being *meaningful*.

Focus on the meaningful, worthwhile aspects of life. It'll be a constant battle, but it'll be one that is worth the fight.

3

Finances

So you've landed your dream job, and within weeks, that paycheck starts rolling in. But before you get too excited, remember that with a full-time job comes more responsibility. With college loans to pay off, a new car to save for because that college one isn't going to kick it forever, along with apartment fees, phone bills, and grocery expenses, it's easy to spend it all before you've even had time to bask in the joy of that glorious check. Even after you embrace a minimalist lifestyle, you will still have bills to pay.

Before blindly signing away your entire month's work, we need to stop, sit back, and think. Below are four steps you need to take to help you manage your finances. These steps will allow you to take control of your finances so you know where every penny of yours is going. Whether you are fresh out of college or counting down the days till you turn thirty, it's time to think about or rethink the way you handle your money.

No matter if you're making $100 per month or $10,000 per month, you need to create a plan. You can never make too much or too little to disregard a spending plan. And I'm not talking about some overcomplicated Dave Ramsey six-week class type of plan or even some phone app type of plan. I've tried those, and they didn't work for me. When a plan is too complicated and intricate, it's easy to give up, "cheat," or feel too overwhelmed to make it past the first week.

So we're going to use a simple budget that can carry you through all of life's curveballs and adventures.

However much you make per month is going to be known as your budget. If you are married, it's best to combine your pay-checks to allow you to optimize your saving efforts. For example, if you make a total income of $3,000 per month, then your overall budget is going to be $3,000. Now we break down this overall budget into smaller areas.

Step 1: Non-negotiable Costs

First, begin by compiling the cost of your necessities. Necessities include rent, utilities, loans, car payments, insurances, and any other non-negotiable payments. You need to know exactly how much you have to pay for those things each month so you don't ever run short. If you're living with a roommate, make sure you are only counting the amount you personally have to pay.

Whenever your paycheck rolls in, set aside money to pay for these necessities. Or try to go and pay them immediately so you don't forget about a payment and think you have more money to spend than you actually do.

Whatever amount you have left in your monthly budget after taking out all of the monthly necessities is what you use for negotiable costs.

Step 2: Negotiable Costs

Whatever money you have left over from your non-negotiable costs is the money you have to use towards flexible costs such as groceries, gym memberships, gas, phone, and whatever else. These costs are dependent on how much you wish to spend.

When deciding how much you're going to spend on negotiable costs, think about how wisely you are spending your money. Do you really need unlimited data on your phone? A $100-per-month gym membership that you're going to use twice? A smorgasbord of food to choose from when you open your cabinets?

As you compile your costs, don't forget to add in contributions or monthly charity donations, because yes, now that you have a full-time job it's time to financially contribute to the rest of society (cue Chapter 2, Step 3!)

Figure out exactly how much you're willing to spend in negotiable areas and let that determine what type of phone you will have, where you will work out, where you shop and well…you get the point. Once you have this down, it's time to get yourself a box of envelopes and learn the six envelopes method.

Step 3: Six Envelopes Method

Here's what you need to do at the beginning of each month. First, pay all of you non-negotiable costs.

Next, set aside six envelopes.

In the first envelope, put your charity donations inside and seal it up until it's time to give away. This will prevent you from skirting in this area or feeling the need to spend this money throughout the month. Since it won't be in your bank account, you won't be tempted to use it. Try to turn it into wherever it goes as soon as you can so, once again, you won't be tempted to use it on other things.

Now, take out four envelopes. These are going to be your weekly envelopes of money for the month. Fill each envelope up with your spending money for the week. This includes grocery money, gas money, restaurant funds, and any other flux money. Be realistic in how much you think you'll spend for that week. And if it's a five-week month, make sure you plan for it.

At the end of every week, you can open up your new envelope of money for the upcoming week. It's like opening up a present for yourself every Friday once the work week ends and a new weekend dawns. I personally open a new envelope every Friday and the money inside must last until the following Thursday.

Use just the amount of money you have allotted for yourself for the week without having to use your card or tap into your savings. And no dipping into the following week's money before it's time! If you can't pay for it with the cash allotted for the week you're on, you don't have the money for it.

Your last envelope is going to be your emergency money. This money is negotiable, and you can set aside however much you would like. I typically set aside $200.

Seal this emergency money up in order to be prepared for worst-case scenarios. This is the money you use when you randomly have to buy new brake pads for your car, when you have to fly out of town for an unexpected funeral, when your toaster dies, or you accidentally go over on your data charges.

The world is a crazy chaotic place where you can't possibly predict all of the variables. You have to be ready for the expenses you can't know are coming your way. Know that chances are something will go wrong each month, and you don't want it to mess up your whole financial structure when it happens. Your grocery money shouldn't have to be used for changing your oil or fixing your vacuum. Set aside money so you'll be prepared for the worst.

If by the end of the month you have extra of this emergency fund, put it towards next months. Call it bad luck or just classic "adulting," but I typically use up the majority of my emergency fund each month.

Using the six envelopes method helps you take control of your money rather than being a slave to a credit card. You will know exactly how much you have spent and how much you have left to spend for the week. If you run out too early, then you'll just have to wait until next week to spend more money. If you have extra at the end of the week, then you can put that towards something else or towards a bigger expense you know you have coming up.

Step 4: Savings

So you've paid your non-negotiable bills. You've set aside your six envelopes. You're ready for the month.

But what about your savings?

Whatever money you have left after setting aside your six envelopes and paying your non-negotiable bills is what goes into the savings account.

Whether you have a few thousand left over or fifty bucks, you need to put it towards your savings. And don't touch it. This is the money you'll use some day to make a down payment on a house or make your first investment. Save this money for as long as you can until it's the right time to spend it. You want this money to multiply so it makes you more money in the coming years.

Now comes the question I know you're all wondering about…what about vacations?

As a twenty-something, you should utilize your youth to travel and see the world. But in order to be able to afford to travel without having to dip into your savings, it's important to set aside money each month for any future trips you want to take.

Consider your vacation funds as your seventh envelope. Except instead of using this money each month, the envelope should be growing thicker each month.

I use any extra money I have from random side jobs such as tutoring, babysitting, and any leftover emergency funds and put it towards my travel budget. The amount of money I have in my vacation fund determines what type of vacation I'll be taking. If it's just a few hundred dollars, then I'll probably be taking a beach trip or snatching up a last-minute cruise deal. If it's a few thousand, I'll be heading to Europe. At different points in life you'll have different amounts of money, so just because you can afford that dream Europe trip one year doesn't mean you can afford it the next year. And vice versa. Be smart, and don't plan a vacation you can't afford.

If you are unable to work side jobs for extra vacation money, you'll have to take out money from your monthly budget and add it to your vacation fund. It can be as much or as little as you'd like. It's typical to take two vacations per year, so plan your budget accordingly.

The key to saving money is by minimizing your costs and, in turn, minimizing your lifestyle. You don't need to have a fully decorated apartment the moment you get your first set of keys. You don't need a new car; ride that old college clunker till it dies. You don't need to go out five times per week when you can make food at home for a fraction of the cost. And you certainly don't need to be buying new clothes, shoes, and other items just for fun.

Use your money wisely. If you're unsure of how to use your money wisely, reread Chapter 2.

As you enter your twenties, you have entered a life where your college friends all have new, different jobs (with various incomes) and your new friends and coworkers may be more established in life than you are. Don't fall into the pressure of keeping up with them. How much they have or what they choose to spend their money on should have no effect on you.

When those around you start to do well financially, be happy for them. Celebrate their wins, but don't let it steal your focus. Focusing on them will only cause you to fall behind.

Striving to keep up with those around you sets a bar for yourself that may very well be unachievable. I know it can be tempting to buy whatever the heck you want as that new, adult paycheck starts to roll in. However there is no need to over complicate our lives with stuff that we may not be able to keep as life continues to change. What happens when we get married and now have to share that over-packed closet? What happens when we get laid off and can no longer afford those new car payments? It's best to keep things simple.

Acquiring things will only lead us to become slaves to the new things we thought would make us happy.

Keep things simple so you can be ready for whatever life has up its sleeve to throw at you.

Take control of your financial situation. If your situation isn't bringing in much dough, it's still important to be on top of it. Know how much you have, how much you can spend, and exactly where your money is going.

As an old Swedish proverb says, "He who buys what he does not need steals from himself."

Don't let your finances take ownership over you. Work with what you have, and in time, your profits will multiply.

4

Fitness

For the longest time, my main goal when working out was to stay skinny. As long as I had slim thighs, a flat tummy, and arms small enough to wrap my hand around, I was happy.

So as I got older and had to stop relying on school sports to keep thin, I ran, biked, swam, and elipticalled—that's a word, right?—in order to maintain my figure.

But soon, my slim legs started getting thicker and my booty started getting bigger. Running and biking were indeed doing the opposite of keeping me slim. I was building muscle, and this was causing me to gain weight.

So naturally, I freaked out.

Why was the scale saying I was heavier now than I was before I started running nine miles per day? Why were my pants getting tighter? Not only that, but I was hungrier…much, much hungrier. So naturally, I started eating more.

Pasta made me run further. Meat made me feel strong. And

those veggies were great, but eating only veggies with my meat didn't keep me full like it used to. It was as though working out intensely was doing the opposite of everything I wanted it to.

But little did I know I was becoming strong.

I voiced my concern to my bodybuilding husband—OK, he's not really a bodybuilder, but anyone who spends two hours in the gym every day is a bodybuilder in my book—and he informed me that muscle weighs more than fat. So by building more muscle, I will burn more calories throughout the day and during my workouts.

I decided to take my husband's word for it and up my workout game to another level.

I added in weights. I cut down those nine-mile runs to just three miles per day.

I added in a solid gym workout to go with my cardio. Each day was devoted to different muscle groups split between my lower body and upper body.

After just a week or two of adding in weights, my body fat percentage was lowered by two percent, and my muscle percentage went from being in the 30s to the 40s.

But my overall weight went up.

Little by little as I gained more and more muscle, my weight crept up. I was painfully aware that muscle does indeed weigh more than fat.

But I didn't let that stop me.

Slowly but surely, I was able to use heavier weights and doing things like running and biking became even easier. A hilly mountain bike ride used to have me huffing and puffing, but now I felt energized and ready to take on the next hill without pausing to rest. Throughout the day, I felt more awake and I didn't slug through my workday anymore, waiting for the coffee to kick in.

Instead, I let the endorphins in my body do their thing. I felt like I could conquer the world…or at least conquer the huge pile of laundry slowly amassing in my guest room.

Having your dream body shouldn't be about getting skinny or getting down to a certain number on the scale. In fact, it's probably best if you toss your scale in the trash. Throw those tape measures away; don't focus on a number.

Focus on becoming the strongest, best version of yourself you can possibly be. And no, becoming strong doesn't mean you're going to look like a crazy ripped bodybuilder.

It just means your body will be toned and have definition. It means you'll be able to open that jar of pickles without having to ask for help.

We're going to go through two simple steps together to help you feel motivated to achieve your body goals. Whether you want to shed a few pounds, gain muscle, lose your gut, tighten those arms, or simply be able to walk up a flight of stairs without feeling winded, these steps will help you achieve just that.

Step 1: Get Active

Exercise? What? That long lost verb you've been avoiding since you graduated high school? It's so very common to enter your twenties and get lost in the sea of working, social engagements, and the tidal wave of responsibilities that hits you once you start having to do things on your own. Exercising often gets pushed to the back burner and slowly but surely you begin to pack on weight.

It's easy to live a sedentary lifestyle. We go to work and sit much of the time. We sit in our cars going to and from work. We come home from work and sit on our couch. We lie down, go to sleep, and do it all over again the next day. If you've ever owned a fitness tracker, I'm sure your painfully aware of how little we Americans actually walk throughout our day.

However, as we go throughout our twenties, the dreaded reality is that at some point our metabolism will start slowing down if it hasn't already. And soon we may have babies and our bodies will grow, change, and have the potential to stay in post-baby form rather than going back to its original size. And none of us wants this to happen. But it will if we don't start taking control of our health now.

The key to becoming strong, empowered young women isn't about just exercising but about becoming active in general. Figure out what you like to do and find a way to get yourself moving. If you like being outside, go on a daily walk with your roommate or significant other. Breathing in the fresh air will expose your body to pathogens and strengthen your immune system, leading you to become a healthy person in more areas than one.

If you enjoy swimming, find a local gym with a swimming pool available for you to use. If you enjoy nature, lace up those boots and go for a hike. If you enjoy riding your bike, get out there and ride! And if you enjoy relaxing and watching television, play a Youtube video on your laptop and get moving in your living room. Don't let business or laziness hold you back from allowing the blood in your veins to get pumping.

Those endorphins I mentioned? You'll feel them. You just have to put yourself into situations that allow you to.

And you don't have to set an unrealistic goal for yourself of running an ultra marathon or completing the Ironman in order to consider yourself active. Setting unrealistic or far-off goals will only cause you to burn out or give up when you realize just how much time and effort it takes to reach those goals. Simply strive to be a little more active than you were yesterday. Soon you'll fall into a habit of being active daily. Remember, habits are what build lifestyles. By striving to build habits that keep your body moving, you will reap the benefits throughout your life.

Step 2: Work Those Muscles

As you start focusing on becoming an active person, soon those stairs become easy to climb. Going for a run might not have you feeling like you're dying, and a game of tennis or racquetball might start to seem fun rather than tiring.

Once you get to this point, you can now take your workout game to another level. It's time to work with those weights. Like I said before, using weights will not have you looking like a man. Instead, working out with weights will improve your ability to perform daily living activities. By using weights, you will burn body fat at an increased rate throughout the day, you will release stress and tension, you'll strengthen your bones, and you'll sharpen your cognitive function. Additionally, you will improve your balance, posture, and coordination. Each of these things will start to deteriorate once you enter your thirties.

Being in your twenties is the only time in your life you can truly allow your body to reach it's fullest potential. Don't let that go to waste. Do it while you still can.

When incorporating weights into your workout routine, it's okay to start light as you get into a routine of lifting. Over time, you can add on more weight.

Set aside three days of your week to devote to weight training. You can still do cardio on these days, but you're going to spend a good thirty to forty-five minutes in the weight room strengthening your muscles.

Start by creating a workout plan. You should have a Leg Day where you work out your lower body. Next should be a Pull Day where you work out your back, biceps, traps, and back head of your deltoids. Finally, you should have a Push Day where you work on your chest, triceps, and the front and middle head of your deltoids. You can do these days in any order you choose, and you can space them out throughout the week, or knock them all out in three sequential days.

Now there's nothing more intimidating than walking into a weight room and having absolutely no idea where to begin. To prevent his from happening, ask someone who works at your gym for help as you get started. Or, you can ask someone who is working out. I promise those big burly men are not as scary as they may look. Most of the time, people in the gym are more than happy to help.

Exercise gives you endorphins. Endorphins make you happy. Happy people just don't shoot their husbands.

Take it from Elle Woods: exercise makes you happy. The gym should be full of happy people! Even if their faces are contorted in all sorts of ways as they lift heavy metal.

Get in there and jump in—don't be shy!

Here is a sample plan to use as you get started on your journey of building your strength. Use this plan every week and you will most definitely see results. Just cross out "Courtney," scribble in your name, and you're ready to go!

Here are a few notes to consider as you review this plan: when you see "6-6-10-12-12" that means do a set of six first, then another set of six, a set of ten, a set of twelve, and finish off with another set of twelve. Wait fifteen seconds between each set. When you see 3 x 12 or similar, that means do three sets with twelve repetitions in each set. Again, make sure to wait at least fifteen seconds or more in between each set. And if you don't understand what these exercises are, ask a fellow gym-goer or Google it. If you're new to weight lifting and don't know what weights to use, it's a good rule of thumb to start with 1- or 15-pound weights.

Courtney's 3-Day Lifting Program

Leg Day

- Weighted squats 6-6-10-12-12
- Weighted lunges 6-6-10-12-12
- Straight leg deadlifts 6-6-10-12-12
- Leg extensions 3 x 12
- Calf raises 3 x 15
- Weighted jump squats 25-50

Push Day

- Dumbbell bench press 6-6-10-12-12
- Seated Arnold press 6-6-10-12-12
- Incline dumbbell flies 3 x 12-15
- Dumbbell tricep extensions 3 x 12
- Dumbbell shoulder raises 3 x 12

Pull Day

- Deadlift rack-pulls 4 x 5
- Seated dumbbell shrugs 6-6-10-12-12
- Lateral pull downs 6-6-10-12-12
- Dumbbell rows "lawn mowers" 6-6-10-12-12
- Incline curls 6-6-10-12-12

- Cable curls 6-6-10-12-12

5

Nutrition

As fitness professional Rebecca Louise says, "Optimal wellness is based on 20% fitness and 80% nutrition."

Now that we've covered the first 20% of how to become healthy twenty-somethings, it's time to learn about the other 80%: food.

The food we eat is what fuels our body throughout the day. Our nutrition can either aid us in our goal of becoming better versions of ourselves or it can halt our progress. Just because we stay active does not mean we can intake whatever foods we want. Rather, taking in proper nutrition can help us achieve our goals faster and lead us to live a longer, healthier life.

Our diet shouldn't be about cutting foods out but instead about replacing unhealthy foods with foods that will nourish our body. We can do this by aiming to eat foods that are rich in protein and high in nutrients.

The best way to replace unhealthy foods with healthier options is to cut out processed foods. This means we need to eat natural, fresh foods. As a general rule, if it comes in a box, it's processed and therefore should not be eaten.

Our food should be as fresh as possible to provide us with an optimal amount of nutrients: less food in the cabinets, more food in the fridge.

We're going to go through each meal of the day to talk about how we can best provide our bodies with the nourishment it needs.

1. Breakfast

When we wake up in the morning, it's important to fuel our body with food to get us through the day. I know you've heard this hundreds of times, but breakfast really is the most important meal of the day. Breakfast kickstarts our metabolism, helping us to burn calories throughout our day. A nutritious breakfast will also help us to have better memory and concentration.

Breakfast replenishes the blood sugar our bodies lost during sleep. So don't skip it! We need food in our system long before lunchtime. However, many breakfast foods that are often marketed as "healthy" contain added sugars, preservatives, and other ingredients that your body doesn't need. This is why it's best to forego cereal, meal bars, and other processed foods and replace them with all-natural foods. Whole wheat toast with peanut butter, fruit smoothies, eggs, and turkey bacon are just a few examples of all-natural foods that will give our bodies just what it needs to start our day.

Replace over-processed, flavored coffee creamer with half and half or milk. Instead of a protein bar, make homemade energy bites. It's important to feed our bodies just what it needs without adding in extra ingredients that will counteract the work we do in the gym.

2. Lunch

Next comes our midday meal. It's important to eat lunch for it provides us with the energy needed to sustain us throughout the afternoon without pulling on the body's reserve. An ideal lunch should consist of a mixture of vitamins, minerals, fat, carbohydrates, and protein.

Carbohydrates are important to give our body energy; however, it's important to watch where our carbs are coming from. According to Catherine Collins of the British Dietetic Association, "Gorging on carbohydrate-rich foods such as white bread, pasta and potatoes will make you sleepy. This is because large bursts of carbohydrates encourage the body to produce serotonin, the chemical which causes lethargy."

Instead, the carbohydrates we eat should be whole grain. Try eating whole grain wraps, pita rounds, or sandwich bread to fuel up. Boiled eggs, chicken, and tuna sandwiches on whole grain bread all contain a low amount of carbohydrates, a good quantity of protein, and a low amount of fat.

Our lunches don't have to be small to keep thin and fit. It's best to eat more wholesome foods than to eat less and find yourself snacking later on in the day.

3. Dinner

After a long day of working, going to school, and pounding it out at the gym, it's normal to come home starving. Rather than surviving off of comfort foods, fast food, or whatever we can find in the fridge, it's important to make a healthy dinner.

Healthy dinners can be as elaborate or as simple as you prefer. Dinner should include vegetables and a low-fat source of protein. Try to stay away from overeating on carbs and focus on eating more vegetables because of their low-calorie and vitamin-rich nature. Since we will be going to sleep not too long after eating, we don't need the energy from the carbs to keep us awake. Choose lean meats such as chicken, turkey, or venison as your main source of protein and fill the rest of your plate with greens and other types of veggies.

4. Snacks

For snacks, toss those pretzel packets, Oreo slims, and 100-calorie packs and replace them with nuts, fresh berries, and other fruits and veggies. Try carrots and low-fat dressing, almonds, celery and peanut butter, an apple, or a pack of raisins—AKA nature's candy! Snacking shouldn't be empty, nutritionless calories to fill our tummies but rather a way to fuel our body to keep us going throughout the day.

Below, you will find a sample two-day meal plan with dinner recipes to go along with them.

Healthy eating doesn't have to complicated. In fact, eating

whole foods that are nourishing to the body can be inexpensive and easy to do.

And just because we eat healthy doesn't mean we can't ever splurge on a comfort meal or dessert. It just means that we have to limit ourselves when doing so. If we never, ever eat anything unhealthy, chances are we will mentally break at some point and fall back into unhealthy eating habits. If we allow ourselves small treats every now and again, we will find ourselves better able to say "no" when temptation occurs.

I personally allow myself one meal per week where I "splurge." This is normally on a date night with my husband. And we can't have a date night without dessert, so I normally have a treat, as well. This gives me something to look forward to throughout the week and knowing I have a meal to splurge on allows me to control my eating habits throughout each day.

Maintaining a healthy lifestyle may seem difficult at first, but I promise it gets easier. As you get moving and fuel your body with nutritious foods, you'll not only maintain a healthy weight, but you'll also feel happier and more motivated to conquer every area of life.

Sample Meal Plans:

Day 1:

Breakfast:
2 slices of toasted honey bread toast with a thin layer of peanut butter on top

Mid-Morning Snack:
Handful of blackberries

Lunch:
2 boiled eggs
Greek yogurt cup
Handful of raw snap peas

Mid-Afternoon Snack:
Sliced apple with peanut butter

Dinner:
Salmon on bed of spinach
Steamed green beans

Day 2:

Breakfast:
Yogurt parfait

Mid-Morning Snack:
Cheese stick

Lunch:
Salad with grilled chicken, romaine lettuce, and low-fat dressing
Baby carrots

Dinner:
Teriyaki chicken stir-fry
Brown rice

Recipes:

Garlic Basil Atlantic Salmon:

1 tablespoon garlic powder
1 tablespoon dried basil
1/2 teaspoon salt
2 tablespoon butter
Salmon filet big enough for two

Simply combine the spices and rub it into the salmon. Melt the butter on medium heat over the stove then add the salmon. Cook for 4 minutes on each side or until the salmon is firm and flaky. Make sure to keep an eye on it so it doesn't burn! Place the salmon on a bed of spinach leaves and serve with steamed veggies. Serves 2-3.

Teriyaki Chicken Stir Fry

1 pound boneless skinless chicken breast
2 heads of broccoli
1 onion
1 cup of snap peas
1 bell pepper (optional)
1/2 bottle of Lawry's Teriyaki 30 minute marinade

Cut fat off of chicken and cut the chicken into 1-inch chunks. Place chicken into a plastic bag or bowl and pour marinade on top until chicken is covered. Marinate for 30 minutes. Chop up the vegetables and place in large frying pan or wok. Pour more of the marinade on top of vegetables and begin to sauté on medium-high, stirring frequently to coat the veggies. Once veggies begin to soften, add in chicken and cook until chicken is cooked through. Pour a splash of marinade as desired. Serve on a bed of brown rice. Serves 2-3.

Yogurt Parfait

3/4 cup of vanilla Greek yogurt
1 tablespoon of honey
1/2 of a pink grapefruit, peeled and cut into chunks
1 teaspoon of lime juice (optional)

Place grapefruit into mason jar or glass. Pour yogurt on top of the grapefruit. Top with honey and lime juice. Serves 1.

Chocolate Peanut Butter Energy Bites

2/3 cup creamy peanut butter
1/2 cup semi-sweet chocolate chips
1 cup old-fashioned oats
1/2 cup ground flax seeds
2 tablespoons of honey

Combine all five ingredients in a bowl, mix them together and place the bowl in the refrigerator for 20 to 30 minutes. Once cool, roll the ingredients into small balls and they're ready to serve. You can store them in the refrigerator for up to a week or longer in the freezer.

6

Relationships

Being in your twenties is the perfect age to form meaningful relationships. In college and high school, most of your friends will be in the same stage of life as you. However, once you enter into the real world, things change. Suddenly you meet people from all walks of life—right around the time you're separated from your old, safe group of friends.

Your twenties can be a tough time. To survive, make sure you reach out to others to find friends who will help you survive, conquer, and enjoy this transformative decade. Friends won't always pop up out of nowhere like they did in high school and college. As you start your career and say goodbye to the friends of your past, it can be difficult to find new friends in the same stage of life as you. In this new season, it's important to be intentional about seeking out relationships.

Say goodbye to sleepovers, late night study sessions, and meet-ups at the mess hall and welcome in the new world of dinners planned in advance, scheduled movie nights, and lunch with your coworkers who just might be thirty years your senior.

This new world of relationships is quite different from what you're probably used to, but it has its perks. First of all, you are able to meet people of various ages and stages in life so your friendship circle will expand to people your mom's age in addition to people your own age and everything in between. Second of all, now that you're all grown (I know you're thinking—HA, grown up, right!) but people are generally more mature which means less petty fights and dumb arguments. Thirdly, now that you're in your twenties and starting your career, you can do awesome things that you might not have been able to do in your younger years such as eating at fancy restaurants, going on vacation, and enjoying the general feeling of not having to worry if you're going to be able to pay next semester's school bill.

The key to being in your twenties and gaining fruitful relationships is to put yourself in a variety of situations where you can meet new people. If you only spend time at work and at home, then your chances of meeting new people are slim. Figure out what you like to do and find others who like to do the same.

When I turned twenty-three and moved to North Carolina to start my second year of teaching, I was terrified that I would have no friends. I had spent the past two years with relatively no close friends who I hung out with regularly and I was ready for a change. Luckily, I was moving to a new city full of plenty of Millennials just like myself.

Upon arriving at this new city, I went to a three-day conference with people who had the same interests as me and my husband. At this conference, we met tons of new people, some of whom were from the area. These new friends of ours invited us to their church where we were able to get involved with a young professionals group. The group met every Sunday, and throughout the week we would meet in small groups. It was here that I was able to connect with like-minded people and build lasting relationships. The girls in my small group were kind and accepting, and they challenged me in more ways than one to better myself as a person.

I look back at how I stumbled upon these friends, and it took being outgoing and not being afraid to go to new places, which in my case was trying out new churches!

A church is a great place to find new friends who will uplift you and hold you to your morals. It's okay to visit a few different churches in order to find one that has a solid group of people in the same stage of life as you. Once you do find one, you'll be glad you spent the time looking.

Another great place to meet new friends is at the gym. Like I said in the chapter before, exercise gives you endorphins, so people at the gym should be happy! Try out new fitness classes and don't be afraid to introduce yourself.

Find places where other young professionals congregate and jump in on the fun. And no, I don't mean go to a bar and meet acquaintances to share a beer with, but rather join a running club, book club, or simply visit your local bookstore or coffee shop. Many local places have meet-ups designed with the purpose of meeting new people.

If you get invited to a party or social gathering, make connections with those around you. You never know who you might click with if you just start by saying hello.

1. A New Type of Friendship

In your twenties, friendships change. You may not ever find a friend who is as good a friend as your college roommate or your high school BFF. Hold on to those gals who cheered you on at your worst, those girls who you bragged about your first kiss to, those girls who you spent hours dreaming about the future with, the girls who called your mom their second mom, and the ones who will always have your back no matter how much time goes by. But don't become discouraged when you don't find another friend just like them.

As we enter our twenties, the women around us start getting married and having babies and their focuses change. Gone are the days when our friends can drop everything to go shopping or skip out on responsibilities to head to the beach because YOLO. Those wild and free days are now replaced with cleaning the house, making yummy dinners, and making sure the family is taken care of. During such times, friendships can fall to the back burner.

If you have friends in these types of situations, don't be upset by their lack of texts and unanswered calls. Simply be patient with them and understand that their life is different from yours. Just because these gals can't always do the things you want to do doesn't mean you shouldn't continue to strive to be their friend. Often times, these are the girls that need friends the most!

If you find yourself in a situation of being a new wife and trying to do the whole homemaker thing, make sure to carve time out of your day to meet a friend for coffee or invite another couple over for dinner. If you're a young mom, try connecting with other moms to help encourage you and add a little more joy to your life.

Don't underestimate the value of friendship. As a wise proverb says, "Two are better than one because they have a good reward for their efforts. For if either falls, his companion can lift him up; but pity the one who falls without another to lift him up."

Find friends who will lift you up when you fall flat on your face. Believe me, it'll happen to all of us eventually. And better yet, be the friend who lifts others up when they fall or when they fail.

Remember, in order to have friends, we must be friendly.

2. The Menfolk

Now I'm sure your thinking: what about boys?

Or maybe you're not thinking that. Maybe you're a strong, independent woman who don't need no man. If so, I'm glad you've realized that you don't need a man to be happy. You don't need a man to make you feel worthy. You don't need a man to love you, to tell you you're beautiful, or to be proud of you. You already are worthy. You are loved and you are beautiful.

And I'm sure there are plenty of people in your life who are immensely proud of you. I mean, you've made it to your twenties, survived those awkward teen years, and are reading a book! You deserve a standing ovation and should feel quite proud of yourself.

Now despite being a strong, independent woman, being in your twenties does happen to be the prime time for finding your significant other.

Maybe you've already found yours! If so, make sure to keep pouring into your husband every day. Marriage is no easy task, and it requires effort to sustain a life long relationship. Give your husband both time and attention, and make sure you both are fully open and honest with each other.

Date nights should be a weekly activity, and you should strive for ways to serve each other. Being married means you get to live with your best friend for the rest of your life! Don't forget that. Be kind to your husband and spend time growing together.

When my husband and I first got married, we both had a variety of different interests. He liked watching UFC fights, going mountain biking, and spending time hiking outside. I, on the other hand, couldn't care less about UFC fights, had never been mountain biking, and liked going for runs outside on the pavement—not so much on the trails. However, rather than frustrating ourselves with our differences, we found things we both loved to do together.

The two of us got married at the ripe old age of twenty and twenty-two, and we lived in a small town in Florida. The only thing we could do for fun that wasn't an hour away was golf. Consequently, my husband refurbished some old golf clubs for us, and we started taking golf lessons. We found ourselves cracking up at each other as we wacked the ball everywhere but the hole and ended up having tons of fun.

Once we moved to North Carolina, I decided to give the whole mountain biking thing a try. Before I knew it, we were going every weekend and having a blast.

While we still have different interests and hobbies, we were able to come together and enjoy new hobbies to do together as a couple.

Being an old married couple doesn't have to be boring or scary. It can be the best time of your life if you simply put in the effort to work on your relationship and have fun together! Your marriage should be the most important relationship in your life, so every minute you pour into your marriage is a minute well spent.

If you're still single and waiting for your Prince Charming, be patient. Don't jump into a relationship because you're lonely or in desperate need of companionship. Be okay with being alone, and enjoy this precious time because once you find someone, you won't get this time of singleness back.

I know that when you're single, the prospect of being married one day can seem like a surreal fantasy that will happen "one day." But stop focusing on this fantasy! That "one day" could be five years from now, and if it is, you don't want to look back on this time and see it as a wasted season where you were discontented with life. Enjoy your singleness! Own it, live it, and love it.

Being single has some major perks. You can do whatever you want, decorate how you wish, and you only have to worry about yourself. You only have to cook for one, you don't have to do double the laundry, and you don't have to deal with having a smelly boy around. More importantly, being single provides you with opportunities you may never have again in your life.

Take a trip with your gal pals. Explore a new country. Deepen your relationship with your family. Work in whatever city you want to work in. Spend time doing the things you absolutely love. Go on dates. Eat, drink, and be merry! Being single is awesome.

Looking back at my own life, I wish I could have spent the years before meeting my husband with a similar mindset. Instead, I spent years flirting with and dating guys who really weren't worth my time when I should have just focused my attention on my family and friends. When my husband did come into the picture, I knew the moment I met him that he was "the one" and I regretted wasting my time pining after those other dudes.

As you seek to find the one who you will spend your life with, take your time and be wise. Make sure the men you date and enter into relationships with are good men. The last thing you want to happen is to enter into a relationship with someone who will cheat on you or leave you down the road, and often times those signs are prevalent long before you get married.

If the guy you're interested in flirts with other girls, doesn't make you a priority, or treats you harshly, then it might be best to let him go. If he doesn't let you have other friends or monopolizes your time, that's a sign he might just be too controlling. If your family or close confidants show hesitation about you dating him, listen to their reasoning and take it into consideration. Chances are, they see aspects of the relationship from a different perspective and want to make sure you are aware of them.

As you date, keep in mind that the man should pursue you. That doesn't mean you can't show interest in him, but it does mean than he should be taking you on dates and striving to get to know you more.

Now that we've entered an age where social media is a thing, many guys have become lazy when it comes to dating. Sending you a picture via the latest app might mean they're interested. Messaging you online means they're ready to get to know you. But many times, that's as far as it goes. They message you and you pour your heart out to this guy behind a screen, but the day he asks you out may never come.

Be hesitant to get to know guys via online messaging or texting. You could spend days, weeks, even months messaging a guy who could lose interest and leave you hanging in the lurch. If a guy is really interested in you, then talking in person should be no big deal. Meeting up for coffee or grabbing food together is a much better way to get to know someone. If you suggest as much and they are hesitant or unwilling to follow through, then let them go. No use wasting your time on someone who won't hang out with you in person.

People can make themselves sound as great as they want behind a screen. However, in person people are often more open and honest. Once you start hanging with a guy in person, you can get to know the real version of them and not just the person they portray themselves to be.

If after a while this guy who you've been "talking" to starts to lose interest or never asks you out on an official date, let him go. Good riddance. Don't try to get him back—he's lost interest and most of the time there's nothing we can do.

If a guy you're talking to does ask you on a date and you've gotten to know him enough to know he might be compatible for you, go out and have fun! Getting to know someone takes time. Just because you go on a date doesn't mean you're going to get married. Stay calm and be rational.

Guard your heart throughout the dating process. You don't want to fall in love with a guy who ends up not meeting your standards, who doesn't share your beliefs, or who treats you poorly. When we fall in love, our caution is often thrown to the wind, and guys we know we shouldn't be with end up being the ones we stay with. Guarding our hearts against falling in love immediately allows us to see the guys we date with a clear, conscious mind.

Normally after the first few dates it becomes obvious if the guy you're dating is what you're looking for in a man. If he doesn't have the qualities you're looking for, don't wait around hoping he will change or that he will suddenly surprise you with qualities you have yet to see. Move on and don't look back.

And if you don't know what qualities you are looking for in a man, it's never too late to make a list of qualities beyond the outer appearance that you find important. This keeps you from falling head over heels with a guy who you'll some day divorce.

Once you get married, the starry-eyed feeling of what the future might hold soon begins to fade. You find yourself married to someone forever and you have to accept them and all their faults. We have to be able to forgive them when they mess up. We have to love them when they fail. We have to support them when they need encouragement. We have to be by their side both literally and figuratively as we walk through life together. We have to love them when it's difficult. We have to show them love, and we have to keep our eyes from wandering. They are our one and only, and there's no going back. Joining into a marital relationship should not be taken lightly.

If you're engaged, first of all, congrats! As you prepare for your big day, it's so easy to forget about preparing for the whole marriage deal as you focus on planning a wedding. Make sure to take the time to spend with just you and your soon-to-be husband where you don't talk about the wedding. Spend time going deeper. Talk about your hopes and dreams of your marriage.

Talk about where you will go to church. Talk about how you will plan out your budget. Talk about how you both want to spend your married weekends. Talk about who will do the chores, who will cook, and how often you want to have friends over. Talk about if and when you will have children. Talk about these important issues so you know you are both on the same page.

If you're not on the same page, you might want to stop and reconsider entering into marriage. The issues that might not seem important now can be monumental a few years down the road once you're already married. It might be absolutely humiliating to end an engagement, but it's better to end it now than suffer through a marriage where you have differing opinions on how you want your life to play out.

One way to bring these topics to the table is by taking part in premarital counseling. This is a way to talk about subjects you might not always think about. A counselor can help guide you through the correct way to fight (because you will fight!) and can help you work through issues now so you don't have to work through them when you're married.

So whether you are single, in a relationship, engaged, or married, focus on where you're at and enjoy this stage of life. In your twenties, your life and your relationships will change in countless ways. Stay focused on your goals, and keep your head on your shoulders.

The people you meet now will be there for you in the decades to follow, and that's what matters most.

7

Travel

The twenties are often said to be the golden window of travel. At this ripe age, we are young, broke, and totally willing to spend a night in a dank hotel, take the cheapest flights, and survive off of hostel breakfasts and cheap dinners.

We love it. We thrive off of it. Whether we're wandering the streets of Europe, exploring the jungles of South America, or navigating our way through the Caribbean islands, we'll take what we can get.

And while our budgets may be low, that doesn't have to stop us. We live in a time where the other side of the world is a short plane ride away. We can go from one side of our country to the other in a matter of days in a car. The planet has never been more accessible than it is now.

With that being said, the prospect of actually applying for a passport, booking a flight, and figuring out how to rent a car can be quite terrifying. So terrifying that we never actually do it. Instead, we fill our Pinterest boards up with places we want to travel but never end up actually going.

But I don't want that to happen to you. I want you to be able to explore somewhere new and get to know another part of the world. If you don't do it now, when will you do it? We say we'll do it later, but later never actually gets here. Make the most of today, the here and now, and in turn, we will be making the most of our lives.

I've come up with a few ways to make travel both affordable and feasible for us twenty-somethings. As you start your career, take control of your finances, and adopt a minimalist lifestyle, you'll soon have the resources to take a trip of your choice. Isn't that a great feeling, knowing that you can travel to anywhere in the world? I know for me it feels rather freeing. And extremely exciting. So we're going to go through three steps that will help you plan out your dream vacation.

Step 1: Timing

The first thing to consider when planning your dream vacation is to decide when to go. Generally, it's much cheaper to fly to places during that place's off season.

Off-seasons vary depending on where you are going. If you are hoping to visit a tropical location, the high season is normally during school breaks, such as summer, winter, and spring break. The off season would be the months in between those school breaks when children are typically in school and families are less likely to take time off to travel.

If you're planning on visiting Europe, the off-season is typically during the winter when it's colder and there are fewer visitors.

And if you're looking into cruising, the costs of cruising during the summer can be double the price of going in the fall!

Deciding on your timing plays a huge part in your vacation planning.

The costs of traveling can vary from week to week and even from day to day. It's best to decide on a general time frame of when you want to travel rather than a specific day so you know you can get the best deal available on your flight and hotel.

Recently, I was planning a trip to Hawaii for my summer vacation. I had the funds ready to book, I had the hotel and airlines picked out, and I had purchased a fair share of travel books which I spent hours pouring over, highlighting, and underlining everything I wanted to see. I mapped out my week long itinerary, calculated the costs of my activities, and even knew which rental car I wanted. I was so ready.

However, that was around the time when I received notice that I would not be returning to my job for a second year of teaching, and I had to find another position. After my husband and I decided we would be moving to a new state, we realized that the week we had blocked out for Hawaii would be the week we would have to move. This meant that our vacation week would have to be pushed back to a later week.

At first, I figured this was no big deal. We hadn't booked anything yet, so moving our vacation back would be no problem. However, that was not the case.

I soon realized that plane tickets and hotel prices to Hawaii were literally double the price on the new week than they were on our old week. And the prices continued to worsen the further into summer we looked.

Sadly, this meant we would not be going to Hawaii. All of the time I spent researching and planning was a huge waste because we could no longer afford it due to our change of schedule. Luckily, I was able to find a great deal in the Bahamas that fit into our budget, so it wasn't a huge loss, but it was still a bummer not being able to travel to the Big Island.

That's why it's important to know your timing before you plan. This way you can plan the rest of your trip accurately and know exactly how much you will be spending.

Once you have done your research on timing and have a general time frame figured out as to when you will go, you can move on to the next step.

Step 2: Planning

Now this is the fun part! Planning where you will go, how you will get there, and what you will see when you're there is definitely one of the most exciting parts of traveling. However, there are a few things you should know before setting your travel bug loose.

First, make sure to book your hotel and flight together. Utilizing sights such as Expedia or American Airlines Vacations can drastically cut down on the overall cost of your trip. Many times when you're booking an expensive flight, the hotel cost is free or highly discounted. Don't make the rookie mistake of booking these two essential parts of your trip separately. Compare prices on various travel sights to find the best price for your trip.

Secondly, figure out how you will get around once you reach your destination. Will you be renting a car, taking the metro, or simply relaxing at a resort with no need for transportation? If you are in need of a car, it is often more cost efficient to book the car on the same site you booked your hotel and flight. And make sure to watch out for hidden conditions and fees such as insurance costs or age limits.

If you plan on traveling around on a subway or metro, do research to decide the most cost efficient way to purchase your train tickets. Is it cheaper to purchase a booklet of tickets or to purchase tickets each time you enter the station? Are there buses around that are even cheaper to use? Knowing this before you travel will save you money and prevent frustration upon arrival.

If you are hoping to utilize a type of taxi service, know how much it should cost you for a ride in one before arriving so you don't end up getting fooled into paying more than you should. Taxi drivers can often take advantage of uninformed tourists, so don't let that happen to you.

Lastly, when you're planning out your activities, make sure you create a daily itinerary before you go. Know what you are going to do each day so you can maximize your vacation time. This doesn't mean you have to fill in every moment of the day with something to do, but it helps to have a general idea of what you want to do so you don't waste valuable time figuring out what to do next.

There's nothing worse than finding yourself in unknown territory not knowing how you should spend your time. Do research before you go. Utilize guidebooks, blogs, and other resources to make sure you don't miss a thing.

Step 3: Traveling & Safety

As you pack up your suitcase and prepare for travel, there are a few things you need to make sure you do.

First, weigh your suitcase to make sure it is under the weight limit. Having to pay fees you didn't plan on paying for because of an overweight suitcase would not be a very happy start to your trip.

One way to cut down on weight is by foregoing travel-sized toiletries. Most hotels offer complimentary toiletries and will keep your bathroom full of such toiletries free of cost. So leave the shampoo, conditioner, and soap at home. Chances are it will probably just end up leaking all over your things anyway. And whatever liquids you do decide to bring, make sure you place them in a plastic bag to prevent leakage from happening.

Next, make sure to carry your money in a money pouch hidden from view. Don't place your money in a book bag, purse, or another area that pickpocketers could target.

When I was in Paris, I found slashes on my husband's book bag days after returning home. This means someone took a razor to his backpack and sliced holes into the bottom, hoping things would fall out so they could take them. Luckily, we had our money safely tucked away on our sides so no funds were stolen. Make sure you take adequate precautions to hide your money.

Lastly, make sure to contact your bank to let them know you will be leaving town. When banks or credit card companies see that your card is being used in a different country or state, they could consider this "suspicious use" and shut down your card. By letting your bank know you are going out of town, this will prevent them from shutting down your card. Even if you plan on using cash the entire trip, it's important to make sure they are aware you will be gone, just in case there is an emergency and you need to use it.

Also contact your local police station or neighborhood watch to let them know that you will be out of town so they will know to keep an eye on your house in case something were to happen. If something does happen to your house while you are away, it's important that the police or neighborhood watch know how to contact you.

So after doing the above steps, you're ready to head off on a new adventure! I would love to guide you along with what to do while you're there, how to keep costs low, and how to avoid culture shock, but unfortunately, you'll just have to figure out those things on your own.

That's the beauty of traveling. As you visit new places and explore different parts of the world, you will be learning throughout your entire journey. You will learn more from traveling than you ever will from any book, television show, or story.

And the same goes for life. The more experiences you have, the more you will learn. The failures you go through and the successes you achieve are all learning processes preparing you for what's next.

As you go through this fantastic, exciting, once-in-a-lifetime trip through your twenties, you will be faced with challenges, obstacles, and seasons that will have you feeling like you're on a roller coaster. And that's okay. You'll get through it all.

You're a smart girl, after all. You'll be just fine.

About the Author

Courtney is a born-and-raised Florida girl learning to survive in East Asia. When she's not tackling new languages and navigating far-away cultures with her husband, Trenton, she can be found writing about her adventures on her blog, courtneylivin.com.

THOUGHT CATALOG Books

Thought Catalog Books is a publishing house owned by The Thought & Expression Company, an independent media group based in Brooklyn, NY. Founded in 2010, we are committed to facilitating thought and expression. We exist to help people become better communicators and listeners in order to engender a more exciting, attentive, and imaginative world.

Visit us on the web at *www.thoughtcatalogbooks.com.*

Collective World

Thought Catalog Books is powered by Collective World, a community of creatives and writers from all over the globe. Join us at *www.collective.world* to connect with interesting people, find inspiration, and share your talent.

www.ingramcontent.com/pod-product-compliance
Lightning Source LLC
Chambersburg PA
CBHW031631040426
42452CB00007B/773